Welcome to Durham Cathedral. Whether you come as pilgrim, art-lover, or are simply curious, we hope that this guide to post-war art helps you to appreciate the recent art in the Cathedral and to gain new insights into the Christian story which it illustrates.

In the Old Testament, craftsmen who were skilled in working with gold, silver, bronze, stone, wood, embroidery and weaving were given the responsibility of creating a beautiful place of worship (Exodus 35:30-35). Christianity welcomes the contribution of the arts in worship where they have a role in illuminating and teaching the Christian faith, in aiding our contemplation of God, and in provoking us to thought and new insights about God which words alone might not suggest.

This Cathedral is itself a work of art, a sacred space built for the glory of God, and over the centuries since it was built, artists and craftsmen have added their contributions. Children entering the Cathedral say "wow" – it takes us out of ourselves and points us to something (Christians say Someone) more wonderful than we have previously imagined. But, in the words of another child visiting the Cathedral, "it sort of wraps its arms around you," and over the centuries this place has welcomed and offered sanctuary to millions of people. It is a prayed-in place that draws us to God.

The art in the Cathedral is not here for its own sake, as in an art gallery, but is part of the fabric of this holy place and is intended to help those who look at it to draw closer to God. This guide book has been written not only to introduce the art and artists, but also to set these in their context within the Christian story of which this Cathedral is itself a part. Some short prayers are included which you may wish to pray as you ponder the art, either here in the Cathedral or using the pictures in this book when you go home.

Art can open up new ways into well-known stories by drawing our attention to things we had not noticed before and can show us the familiar in a different guise. So, as you walk round the Cathedral, take time to look at the works of art and ponder what you see. Begin at the west end of the Cathedral, in the Galilee Chapel, with the statue of the Annunciation which marks the beginning of the Christian story and then gradually move east until you end at St Cuthbert's shrine with Christ reigning in glory, anticipating our future hope as Christians. You may want to take this book home and use it in your prayers, letting God speak to you afresh as you look at the pictures and read the biblical stories mentioned here.

The Cathedral is a place of worship and sanctuary and we ask that, in order to avoid disturbing other people who have come for many different reasons, including seeking quiet and trying to maintain anonymity, you do not take photographs, instead, postcards and CDs of many of the pieces are available in the Cathedral shop.

The Revd Canon Rosalind Brown
September 2010

The portrayal of the Christian story in art in Durham Cathedral begins in the Galilee Chapel with the statue of the Annunciation by Josef Pyrz. The story of the annunciation, when the Angel Gabriel told Mary that God had chosen her to be the mother of his Son, is found in the Gospel of St Luke (Luke 1:26-38) and is one of the most popular scenes in Christian art. Most artistic representations of the Annunciation show both Mary and Gabriel and portray a vivid range of emotions in both characters. But here in Durham, only Mary is portrayed and she stands serene, nearly life size and erect like one of the slender pillars.

The artist says that he has shown Mary as 'Everywoman', although most people see a young African girl. Her face is carved realistically and conveys the message of her peaceful acceptance of the angel's startling message: the smooth openness of the hollow of her body represents her openness to God, with the hint of the child growing within her. But feel the back of her neck: it is ridged, due to the tension that has built up there.

The sculptor has captured the way that there is a tension inherer in any calling from God, which comes as both promise and challenge.

Running one's fingers over the roughness of th ridges at the back of the neck, whilst also looking at the prayerful serenity epitomised in Mary's face, can be a catalyst for prayer for anyone who faces seemingly impossible demands in life and needs the assurance that God is in the midst of the situation.

Josef Pyrz was born in 1946 in Gowolowak, Poland. In 1979 he left h homeland for voluntary exile in France in order to secure his artistic freedom. This carving, *Annunciation 2*, is made from ash and Pyrz has worked with the grain and gnarls of the wood t convey the sense of peac and of spiritual yearning It was the artist's wish that it should be placed in a Romanesque Cathedral and he saw it in the Galilee Chapel in 2000. The sculpture was a gift in 1992 of the Jerusalem Trust and an anonymous donor.

Lord Jesus Christ, your mother Mary said "yes" to G Help me to say "yes", knowing that you are with me, and help me to trust you even when the way ahead seems hard. Amen.

2. The Stella Maris Window

This *Mary, Star of the Sea* window in the north-east corner of the Galilee Chapel complements the statue of Mary; both being particularly appropriate since the Cathedral is dedicated to Blessed Mary the Virgin and the Galilee Chapel was added as the Lady Chapel when women could not enter the main part of the Cathedral.

The window relies on the use of symbolism and shows, on the right, Christ's ministry in Galilee represented by the Chi-Rho symbol for Christ, which is a monogram of the first two letters of his name in Greek.

The left-hand light represents Mary, symbolised by her crowned initial and by two flowers. The lily represents purity and the cyclamen, which has a red spot at the heart of the flower, can be taken to express her sorrows. The burning bush is from the story in Exodus where God called to Moses out of a burning bush that was not consumed by the fire and illustrates both God, who cannot be consumed, and Mary who bore Christ, without herself being destroyed by the fire of God's love. The descending dove is the Holy Spirit who descended on Christ at his baptism and on Mary and the other disciples on the day of Pentecost.

On the right, the thistle of Palestine points to the crown of thorns at Christ's crucifixion. Beside the star, there is a small fish with tribute money in its mouth, an allusion to the incident when Jesus told Peter to catch a fish and he would find a coin in its mouth which could be used to pay tribute to Caesar without implying that Jesus owed him allegiance (Matthew 17:24-27).

The artist said that he thought children would like looking for the fish. At the time the window was installed there was a tree behind the purple area which represents the Sea of Galilee. When the tree blew in the wind, the effect was of movement on the sea.

The designer, Leonard Evetts (1909-1997), lived in Woolsington, and was Head of Design at Kings College, Newcastle. He was influenced by his father's love of architecture, painting and lettering and began his creative work early: if he and his brother broke a window playing football, they replaced the glass using scraps from their father's workshops before he found out! He was also an admirer of the Arts and Crafts movement and placed great emphasis on craftsmanship. He is known as a stained glass artist and a water colourist and continued undertaking stained glass commissions after his retirement, especially in churches in the Northumberland and Durham including St Nicholas' Church, Bishopwearmouth, which has 46 windows by him. He was awarded a Lambeth Doctorate by the Archbishop of Canterbury in 1995. This window, made when he was in his eighties, was donated by the American Friends of Durham Cathedral to celebrate the 900th anniversary of the commencement of building of this Cathedral in 1093.

Lord, thank you for the creativity of artists who illuminate familiar stories in new ways. Thank you for the creative gifts you have given me; may I find new ways to use them to your glory and for the benefit of other people. Amen.

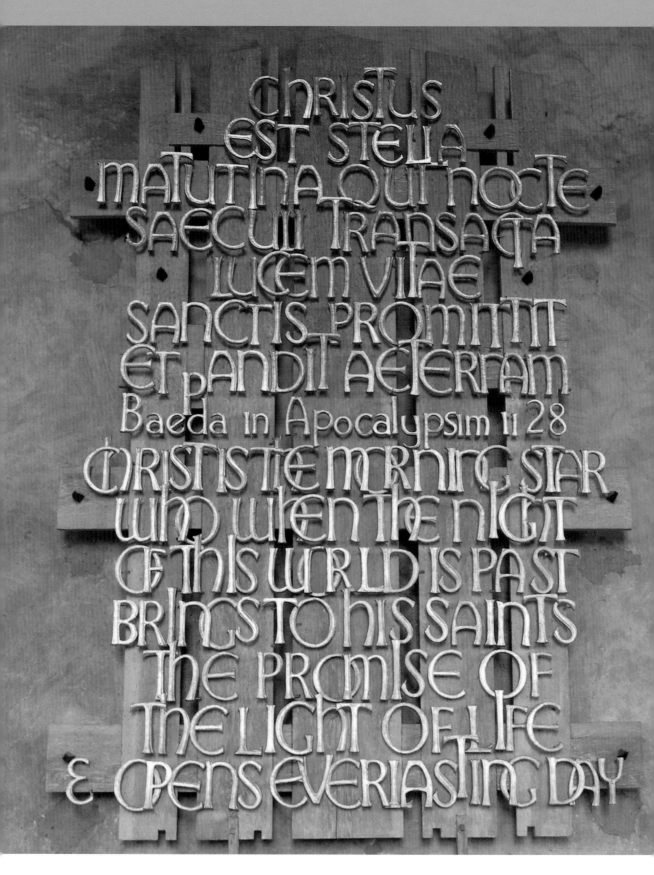

CHRISTUS
EST STELLA
MATUTINA QUI NOCTE
SAECULI TRANSACTA
LUCEM VITAE
SANCTIS PROMITTIT
ET PANDIT AETERNAM
Baeda in Apocalypsim ii 28
CHRIST IS THE MORNING STAR
WHO WHEN THE NIGHT
OF THIS WORLD IS PAST
BRINGS TO HIS SAINTS
THE PROMISE OF
THE LIGHT OF LIFE
& OPENS EVERLASTING DAY

The Venerable Bede was born around 672-673 and, aged seven, entered the monastery at Wearmouth. There, he was educated by the scholar and bishop, Benedict Biscop and later by Ceolfrith, with whom he moved to the new sister monastery at Jarrow, which was founded in 682. Bede and Ceolfrith were the only two survivors of a plague in 686, and maintained the monastic cycle of prayer.

Bede was ordained deacon in about 692 and priest in 702. He wrote his first book in 701. He rarely left Jarrow but, drawing on Benedict Biscop's library of 300 to 500 books, he became the greatest scholar of his age.

The designer was George Pace (1915-1975) and the letter-working was by metalworker Frank Roper (1914-2000). Pace's work can be seen elsewhere in the Cathedral, including the clear glass windows in the north Nave and the entrance porches at the north and south doors of the Cathedral. Echoes of Charles Rennie Macintosh and William Morris can be seen in his designs and he placed great emphasis on craftsmanship. Roper was born in Haworth in Yorkshire and taught in Lincoln, Sheffield and Cardiff where he was Vice Principal of the School of Art. He worked with George Pace in several Cathedrals, and also with Jacob Epstein and John Piper.

Bede was a teacher as well as a writer; he enjoyed music and was a good singer. His writings embraced science, astronomy, grammar, history, poetry, biblical studies, music and theology. He knew Greek and Hebrew. We are indebted to him for most of what we know about the other Northern Saints through *An Ecclesiastical History of the English People* which he completed in about 731. He also wrote two lives of Cuthbert.

Bede died on 26th May 735 while dictating his commentary on St John's Gospel. He had reached chapter 6 verse 9, the story of the feeding of the five thousand. When commemorating him each year in the Cathedral we stop the reading at that point with Andrew's question about the five loaves and two fish, "But what are these among so many people?"

Bede's remains were brought to Durham in about 1020 by a monk who had taken them from the monastery at Jarrow and they are buried in the Galilee Chapel. In 1970, words taken from Bede's Apocalypse were placed on the east wall of the Chapel in Latin and English in memory of Cyril Alington, Dean of the Cathedral from 1933-51, and his wife Hester.

Above the shrine burns an eternal flame, set in a polished brass lantern with a six-pointed star under the base of the glass. Tongues of flame rise from the upper rim, all under the umbrella of the Star of David. The underside of the Star of David has multi-faceted ribs derived from the architectural form of the arches in the Galilee Chapel. Hanging a perpetual light to designate a holy place is a long-established tradition in the Church; the light symbolises Christ, the Light of the world, and reminds us that we, shining as lights in this world, share the inheritance of the saints in light. The light also reflects Bede's words on the Alington memorial. The eternal flame was given by Rotary International to mark their centenary in 2005 and was designed by the Cathedral Architect, Christopher Downs.

The kneeler at Bede's tomb was designed by Joan Freeman, based on the title page from the Lindisfarne Gospels.

Alan Younger's Bede window in the north side of Galilee Chapel commemorates the 1300th anniversary of the birth of the Venerable Bede in 672/3. There is much detail within the window: look carefully and you will find images of Bede; Aidan on his horse; Bede's two teachers, Benedict Biscop and Ceolfrith; and the names 'Jarrow' and 'Wearmouth', the monasteries where Bede spent his life.

It is possible that Younger was influenced by Bishop Lightfoot's suggestion that the Celtic and Roman Churches were brought together in Bede – the left light focuses on the Irish Church with the Dove, symbol of the Holy Spirit, at the top, and the right, with the keys of St Peter at the top, on the Continental Roman Church. The central light focuses on Bede himself, showing him at his studies. Lilan Groves, one of the Cathedral Guides, thinks that the chalice in the left-hand light may represent Cuthbert who, Bede tells us, was often moved to tears when celebrating the Eucharist.

Alan Younger (1933-2004) was committed to preserving the traditions and skills of stained glass work. His designs in numerous medieval churches, St Alban's Abbey and Westminster Abbey, are marked by bold use of colour and are strikingly modern. He cut and painted all the glass himself in his studio in his garden near Crystal Palace, letting details of the design emerge as he worked and rising to the challenges that were presented as the work progressed.

He did much to promote the craft of stained glass in the twentieth century and was Vice President of the British Society of Master Glass Painters.

Also in the Galilee Chapel, the kneelers around the Galilee Altar were designed by Leonard Childs in 2001. They pick up the designs and colours in the fragment of medieval frescoes on the soffit of the arch above the Galilee Chapel altar. Further kneelers, also worked by the Cathedral Broderers, were subsequently provided in the pews by the Galilee Altar.

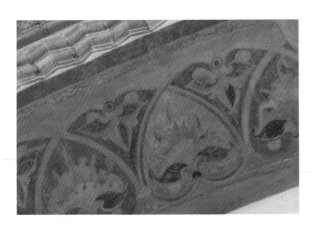

Christ, the morning star, when the night of this world is past, bring to us the promise of the light of life and open to us everlasting day. Amen

Colin Wilbourn's *Last Supper* table was created in 1987 when he was Artist in Residence in the Cathedral. Educated at the University of Newcastle, he has worked since then in the North-East. Following his residency, he created a large outdoor sculpture, *The Upper Room*, which depicted the scene of Christ's Last Supper in the upper room of a house.

This complementary sculpture, in the Galilee Chapel, was mostly made from 500-year-old oak that was removed from the Cathedral bell tower during restoration work.

When closed, it shows a small table set with a platter of bread and a jug of wine but it opens out to provide a flat table surface and is used as the altar table each year during the Maundy Thursday Eucharist in the Cathedral Quire.

The story that it illustrates is that of the Last Supper which Jesus shared with his friends on the night before he was betrayed. This took place in an upper room at the beginning of the Jewish Passover celebrations. During the meal, Jesus took the bread, blessed and broke it and gave it to his disciples, telling them, "This is my body which is given for you. Do this in remembrance of me". Then he took the cup of wine and said "This cup that is poured out for you is the new covenant in my blood" (Luke 22:14-20). Through the centuries since then, in the Eucharist ('thanksgiving') which is at the heart of Christian worship, Christians have taken bread and wine, and followed Christ's example in blessing, breaking and sharing them. The Eucharist is a foretaste of the heavenly banquet in God's kingdom of justice and peace.

This work of art was purchased using bequests given in memory of a former Dean of Durham Cathedral, the Very Revd Peter Baelz - who did much to encourage the visual arts in the Cathedral - and a former Master of Grey College, Mr Victor Watts.

Lord Jesus Christ, as you feed and nurture us, so may we give ourselves to serve you in your world. Send us out to love and serve you in the midst of daily life. Amen.

At the west end of the Nave, the south window by Hugh Easton shows St Oswald, King of Northumbria, holding his sword aloft, echoing the cross beneath it which is the cross at Heavenfield where Oswald was killed fighting pagans.

The Heavenfield cross is surrounded by standing figures, one of whom has a similar pose to St Oswald. The implication is clear – Oswald's sword is as much a sign of his profound Christian faith as it is a sword for battle. It was also, as was the cross for Christ, the means of his death.

At the base of the window there is a memorial to Patrick Alington - the son of Cyril Alington who was Dean of Durham from 1933-51- who died serving as a Captain in the Grenadier Guards in 1943.

On the north side, St Cuthbert, dressed as a bishop, is depicted in the sea, surrounded by a halo of terns, puffins and kittiwakes, in reference to his residence on Inner Farne. This window was damaged in a gale on 13th January 1984 and was repaired by Mike Davies of Brandon Village in a similar style to the original.

Both windows were given by the Friends of Durham Cathedral in 1939 but their installation was delayed until 1945 and thus they are the first examples of post-war art in Durham Cathedral.

Hugh Easton (1906-1965) is responsible for several windows in this Cathedral. The son of a doctor, he worked in Cambridge and London. His work often features substantial areas of undecorated glass that make the figures more prominent. This distinctive design approach can be seen in his St Cuthbert and St Oswald windows, in contrast to the more heavily illustrated background of his RAF window next to St Cuthbert.

We give thanks for the heritage of the Northern Saints. May we follow their example of love for you and care for the welfare of others. In Jesus' name we pray. Amen.

AS BIRDS FLYING
SO SHALL The LORD OF HOSTS PROTECT JERUSALEM

The RAF window is in the north-west corner of the Nave above the Cathedral's war memorial. It was unveiled on 8th April 1948 by Henry, Duke of Gloucester, and serves as a reminder of the then very recent Second World War. The window was designed by Hugh Easton who, before the war, had been responsible for the window in the North Transept which commemorates St Gregory Nazianzen, the fourth century Cappadocian Father; the Chapter House windows; and the Oswald and Cuthbert windows described on the previous page.

Easton was noted for the realism of his war memorial windows including those in Westminster Abbey and the Royal Air Force Memorial Chapel of Remembrance at Biggin Hill. In the Durham RAF window, the face of the central figure, a kneeling airman being taken into paradise, is that of an actual war hero. He rises on the wings of an eagle above a realistic depiction of the city of Durham with the Cathedral and Castle and rows of terraced houses. The text is Isaiah 31:5, "As birds flying, so shall the Lord of Hosts protect Jerusalem". During the war the Canons made a promise, rather like that of Hannah when asking the Lord for the gift of a son (1 Samuel 1:11), that if the Cathedral survived the war without being bombed, they would install a window in gratitude to the RAF. The threat of aerial bombardment was real, and on one night it was only averted by a mist rising from the river to conceal the Cathedral brought about, locals believe, through the influence of St Cuthbert.

Lord, we pray for people in lands that are torn by war; the innocent victims of war; and those who work to bring peace and justice in your world. Protect and strengthen them, we pray. Amen.

8. The Daily Bread window

The title of this window comes from the Lord's Prayer, "Give us this day our daily bread" and the window is an aerial, abstract interpretation of Jesus sharing his Last Supper with his disciples, gathered around a long table with pieces of bread upon it. One figure pulls back very slightly – the artist intended this to be Judas, who left the supper table and went to betray Jesus to the authorities. Then he led their soldiers to arrest Jesus in the Garden of Gethsemane to which Jesus had gone at the end of the meal.

The window was given by the Durham branch of Marks and Spencer to mark the centenary of the business in 1984, the theme of daily bread being a shared one with the Cathedral. The artist is Mark Angus and this window was only his seventh commission; he has subsequently created over 300 windows. He works with mouth-blown flashed glass, and uses glass painting, staining, etching and lead lines. He makes strong use of colour and says his windows don't close themselves to meaning but convey a relevant but not random contemporary message without abandoning mystery, wonder and doubt.

This window embodies narrative but is open to interpretation and the discovery of meaning: where would we place ourselves around this table? Do we pull back from discipleship at times?

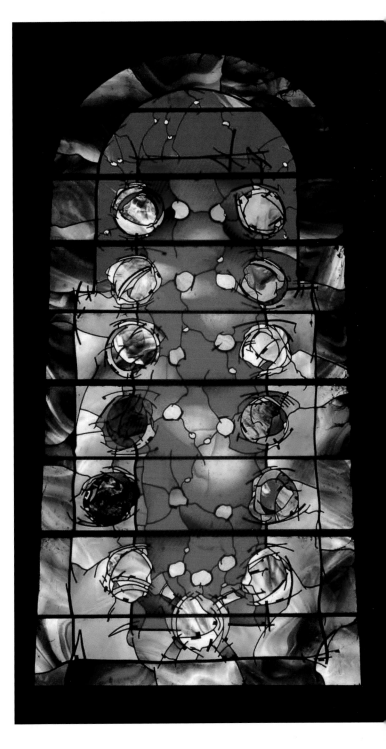

 Lord Jesus, you know the pain of betrayal by a close friend. We pray for people who today share that experience. Help us to be faithful and supportive in our friendships. We ask this in your name. Amen.

9. The Miners' Memorial

Mining has long been a part of the life of County Durham, and the association between the miners and the Cathedral is strong. Bishop Westcott, Bishop of Durham from 1889-1901, was known as the Miners' Bishop and his successor Bishop Moule went into the mines. Although the last pit closed in the 1990s, the annual Miners' Gala is still held in Durham and the Miners' Gala Service fills the Cathedral with mining communities bringing their new banners to be dedicated, accompanied by their brass bands.

The Miners' Memorial was created in 1947 as a symbol of this long association of Durham Cathedral with the mining industry. It looks old because it is made from wood from Cosin's seventeenth century organ screen. This part of the screen had been given in the early 19th century to the Pembertons who lived at Ramside Hall and they used it as a fireplace. When the Cathedral proposed a miners' memorial they gave it back, saying the Cathedral could have "their fireplace".

It reminds us of the human cost of mining because it serves as the memorial for miners who have lost their lives in pit accidents.

The memorial book lists the people killed in pit accidents. A miner's lamp hangs above the book, echoing Christ's words, "I am the light of the world" (John 8:12) and the opening to St John's Gospel, "The light shines in the darkness and the darkness did not overcome it" (John 1:5). The inscription on the memorial, "Remember before God the Durham miners who have given their lives in the pits of this country and those who work in darkness and danger today" were set to music and the anthem was first sung as an act of remembrance at the Miners' Gala Service in 2007.

Remember, O Lord, the Durham miners who have given their lives in the pits of this country, and those who work in darkness and danger today. Amen.

10. The Choir Stalls

Christians have always sung in worship and the choir stalls are used every week in the Cathedral. The Bible includes many hymns and psalms which have been sung in worship through the centuries and there is a lively tradition of hymn-writing and composition in the Cathedral today.

You are invited to join us for worship; there are services every weekday evening at 5.15pm and on Sundays at 10.00am, 11.15am and 3.30pm and normally these include music. There are said services at 8.45am and 12.30pm every weekday.

The Nave choir stalls were designed by Christopher Downs, who incorporated the design of some of the pillars in the Cathedral. Made by the Cathedral craftsmen and paid for by the Friends of the Cathedral, these stalls were dedicated on 8th July 2009. During the week, they are stored in the two transepts and the North Quire Aisle.

Praise the Lord! How good it is to sing praises to our God; for he is gracious and a song of praise is fitting. Sing to the Lord with thanksgiving; make melody to our God. (Psalm 147)

11. The Lesotho Banner

The Lesotho Banner was a gift from the Diocese of Lesotho in 1993 to mark the 900th anniversary of the Diocese of Durham. The materials were paid for by the City of Durham, since the Diocese of Lesotho could not afford them. The two dioceses are linked and there are regular visits by members of each to the other.

The banner shows scenes from Lesotho, which is known as "The Mountain Kingdom" and is one of the smallest and poorest countries the world. This banner reminds us that Christianity is a world-wide religion and is vibrant in Africa.

Lord God [Morena Molimo], thank you for the link between your people in Durham and in Lesotho. We praise you for faith and perseverance through bad times and good. Help us to learn from one another. Keep us all in your love and grace as we work towards justice and peace and the coming of your kingdom; through Jesus Christ our Lord. Amen.

12. St Gregory window

In the fourth century, there was a flowering of theological study in Cappadocia, (part of modern Turkey), particularly associated with Basil the Great, his brother, Gregory of Nyssa, their sister Macrina, and Gregory Nazianzen (330-389). These theologians and church leaders were responsible for the development of the doctrine of the Trinity: that God is Three Persons in One God.

Gregory Nazianzen was, reluctantly, consecrated Bishop but eventually in 375 withdrew to a monastery. With the rise of the Arian heresy, Gregory emerged as one of the leading orthodox theologians of his day and was persuaded to become Bishop of Constantinople. However, church administration was not his real calling and again he withdrew, ending his life working as a theologian and writer, being remembered particularly for his contribution to Trinitarian theology through his writing about the Holy Spirit.

The Chapel in the North Transept is dedicated to St Gregory, hence the St Gregory Window. It includes a quotation, "Thy attuning teacheth the choir of the worlds to adore thee in musical

silence" and a Greek quotation "to eternity". This echoes the words of God to Job that "the morning stars sang together and all the heavenly beings shouted for joy" when God began creating the world (Job 38:7).

This idea is also reflected one of the prayers we use at the Eucharist which includes the words "all your works echo the silent music of your praise".

Praise the Lord from the heavens; praise him, sun and moon, praise him all yo shining stars! Praise him you highest heavens, and you waters above the heav Praise the Lord from the earth, for his name alone is exalted, his glory is above earth and heaven. (Psalm 148: 1,3,7,13)

Jesus was born in Bethlehem. Luke's gospel tells us that, because the city was crowded, there was no available accommodation in an inn, so Jesus was born in a stable. This was part of the house and was where the animals were kept at night. They would have had more privacy there.

Luke's gospel also tells of a visit from shepherds - outcasts in their society since their work prevented them from observing religious laws - who had seen a vision of angels when they were on the hillside at night and had been told of the birth of a saviour. They hurried to visit the baby and found him lying in the manger.

Matthew's Gospel records a separate story - taking place some time later when Mary and Joseph had moved into a house - of a visit from wise men from the East, possibly astronomers, who had seen a new star and interpreted it to mean that a new king had been born.

Despite tradition, they were not kings and we do not know how many of them there were. We know only that they brought three gifts – gold, frankincense and myrrh – all symbolic gifts for a baby who was both

human and divine (gold for a king), and would one day suffer and die (myrrh and frankincense).

The Cathedral's crib figures were carved by Michael Doyle, a retired pitman from Houghton-le-Spring, in 1975 and 1976 using seasoned oak from Raby. Although not a professional wood carver, Doyle discovered his natural gift when whittling spare pieces of wood during rest periods underground. He created the crib figures when well into his seventies without drawings or other help.

The main figures were carved in less than three months without a mistake or spoiled piece of wood. A further supply of wood was used for the wise men.

There are allusions to the mining industry: the ass is a pit pony with its harness and trappings. The crib is a 'choppie box' used to feed the ponies underground. The Innkeeper, depicted on one knee, is dressed as a miner with a water bottle in his pocket, while the dog is a whippet, the miners' constant companion and a local racer.

Joseph's trade is shown in the bag of carpenter's tools and the shepherd supposedly looks like Lord Barnard who gave the wood. Michael Doyle always maintained, with a twinkle in his eye, that this was pure coincidence.

These crib figures have been used each year since 1976. The references to mining remind us of what has been lost to the Durham area. The skill of a craftsman combines with Christian love and reverence to create a crib scene that is unique to Durham.

What can I give him, poor as I am?
If I were a shepherd I would bring a lamb.
If I were a wise man I would do my part,
Yet what I can I give him – give my heart. Amen.
(Christina Rosetti)

The pulpit fall in the Quire portrays the four evangelists using symbolism derived from the Bible: Matthew's man, representing the humanity of Jesus that is expressed in the genealogy at the beginning of the gospel; Mark's lion, reflecting his gospel's beginning, when John the Baptist roars like a lion as he calls people to repentence in the wilderness; the ox of St Luke, representing strength and service as Jesus is portrayed by Luke as offering sacrificial service to the people he meets; and St John's eagle which traditionally was believed to be able to look into the sun, since that gospel soars to the heavenly heights with the story of Jesus' divinity as well as his humanity, and dares to gaze into the purposes of God. The angels' wings unite the four evangelists around the Chi-Rho symbol, which uses the first two letters of Christ's name to speak of his divinity. The first use of these symbols for the four evangelists was by Irenaeus, a Greek theologian of the second century, drawing on imagery in Ezekiel 1:1-14 and Revelation 4:6-7.

The pulpit fall was designed by Leonard Childs (1943-2004) who also designed the Aidan altar frontal. He inherited his skill with scissors and needle from his mother and grandmother but was not formally trained as a textile artist. Instead, influenced by them and John Piper's work at Coventry Cathedral, he became a priest-artist. In the 1970s, he led and worked with an embroiderers' workshop at Derby Cathedral where, in 2002, he was made a Canon. He became known as a designer of church vestments, many of which were tragically destroyed in a fire in Derby Cathedral in 2004. He was preparing to begin over again when he died.

The pulpit fall was the gift of the Cathedral Broderers in memory of two of their members, Joan Finlinson and Joyce Hawkings. They worked it in pure gold and pure silk thread. The pink-purple colour of the fabric picks up the colour in the Scott pavement in the Quire, with cloth of gold for the circles on which the heads of the apostles were embroidered in black silk thread. It was dedicated on 27th February 2000.

Lord Jesus, open our ears to hear and understand you as we read the Bible. Bless all people who preach and teach, we pray. Amen.

The first book of the Bible, Genesis, tells us in stories full of poetic imagery that God created the world and charged humans to care for it responsibly. Human sin not only separates us from God but distorts our relationship with God's world and we have sadly failed in our care of creation. Because the physical creation is integral to God's loving purposes for all creation, God chose to enter it – born as a baby, Jesus, in an occupied country where ordinary living was difficult. Jesus had a different relationship with creation which foreshadows its healing and restoration: he stilled violent storms, walked on water, multiplied food resources to feed the hungry crowd and there was an earthquake when he died on the cross. God's ultimate purposes include the restoration of creation to its intended wholeness and glory, and the final book in the bible brings the story full circle, ending with its poetic imagery of the new creation.

All creation is caught up in God's good purposes for the world; it is not only that we humans are offered new life through the death and resurrection of Jesus Christ, but all creation is healed and restored.

This theological concept is illustrated in the *New Creation altar frontal* by Sally Greaves-Lord which was dedicated in 2009. It shows the glowing rising sun in a turquoise morning sky, its golden rays penetrating to and animating the extremities of creation. It rises out of the background blue, as if to remind us of Advent and waiting for God's purposes to be fulfilled because the birth of Jesus is the beginning of our world's redemption, the dawning of the light. The sun has yet to rise completely and fill the sky.

Across the frontal is a thin red arc, almost invisible until you come close to it, the thread of pain and passion stitched across glory; the destiny of Jesus, born in Bethlehem and crucified at Calvary.

For Christians, every Sunday - the first day of the week - is a day to celebrate the cross and resurrection of Jesus Christ, while remembering those people who, in their pain and passion, still wait for deliverance.

Sally Greaves-Lord lives in North Yorkshire. Her fascination with textiles began at an early age and was nurtured when living and working in Japan, where her work is very popular. Her innovative work on silk and cotton, which involves dying, painting and printing, is influenced by Japanese banners. This work is digitally printed on silk satin and appliquéd with gold tissue dupion silk.

Thank you, Lord, for the beauty of your creation. Make us wise and careful stewards of it as we anticipate with joy the coming of your kingdom on earth as it is in heaven. Amen.

16. Lam'a Sabach'thani

Jesus was crucified on a cross, a horrific form of torture used by the Romans. This sculpture shows Jesus' body arching away from the cross, perhaps in the agony of pain and the tragedy of abandonment, but his slightly raised head hints at the hope of resurrection. The sandstone base represents the hill of Calvary. At the foot of the cross the representations of an axe head and a skull, items traditionally placed at the foot of crucifixes, represent the last judgement and the medieval legend that the cross of Jesus was placed on the grave of Adam, thus undoing the effects of Adam's sin which has led to human separation from God. Jesus suffered that same separation from God in his death and the title of the sculpture, *Lam'a Sabach'thani*, comes from the words cried loudly by Jesus just before he died on the cross, which are recorded in Aramaic in St Matthew's Gospel, "Eli, Eli, Lam'a Sabach'thani", "My God, my God, why have you forsaken me?" (Matthew 27:46).

This sculpture by the Russian Sculptor Kirill Sokolov (1930-2004) was donated to Durham Cathedral in 2006 by his widow, Dr Avril Pyman. It is made of wood, bone, iron and stone and was cast in bronze by Eden Jolly of Scottish Sculpture Workshops in 1997.

This is an unusual sculpture given that the artist was a member of the Russian Orthodox Church, since it is Western in its conception. The Orthodox Church makes little use of three-dimensional sculpture and normally represents the cross with eight points. There is, however, something appropriate about its location adjacent to the Hild Altar in the Chapel of the Nine Altars where the iconography is reversed and a Western saint is portrayed in a contemporary Eastern icon. The dedication of the sculpture on 20th May 2007 was attended by representatives of the Orthodox Church and the Cathedral Choir sang John Tavener's 'Kontakion'.

Kirill Sokolov was born and grew up in Moscow. His father spent five years in labour camps. His background influenced his work, and he said that it taught him to know fear. He entered art school because it brought extra rations in a hungry city, but he developed an artistic vocation and worked in a variety of media.

In 1963, when the Stalinist marriage laws were repealed, he and Avril Pyman, one of the first British postgraduate students to study in the USSR, entered into the first foreign marriage sanctioned by Khrushchev.

They moved to Northumberland in 1974 during the Brezhnev regime's pressure on artists, but Sokolov found it hard to adjust to English life. They then moved to Durham after a fire destroyed nearly all his works in 1981. After the fall of the Soviet Union, he was welcomed back to Moscow.

He died in 2004, and his obituary in The Guardian said he regarded life as essentially tragic so he celebrated anything that could be rescued from the nightmare and saw art as a kind of salvation, a reaffirmation of an innate Russian faith that Stalin had never managed to erase: he was a Modernist painter who fooled the Soviet authorities with Orthodox art.

All these formative experiences are expressed in the arched body of Jesus on the cross and the title of the piece with its reference to being forsaken.

Sokolov loved this Cathedral, which often featured in his silk-screens, linocuts and paintings, and frequently attended services here. It is appropriate that an Anglican Cathedral should provide a home for the work of an Orthodox artist who, through his art, transcended both national and ecclesiological boundaries.

This sculpture gives powerful and poignant expression to the suffering of people at the hands of oppressors and reminds us that we can bring our pain and that of the world to Jesus in prayer, knowing that he understands it.

When I survey the wondrous cross on which the Prince of Glory died,
My richest gain I count but loss and pour contempt on all my pride.
Were the whole realm of nature mine, that were an offering far too small;
Love so amazing, so divine, demands my soul, my life, my all. Amen (Isaac Watts)

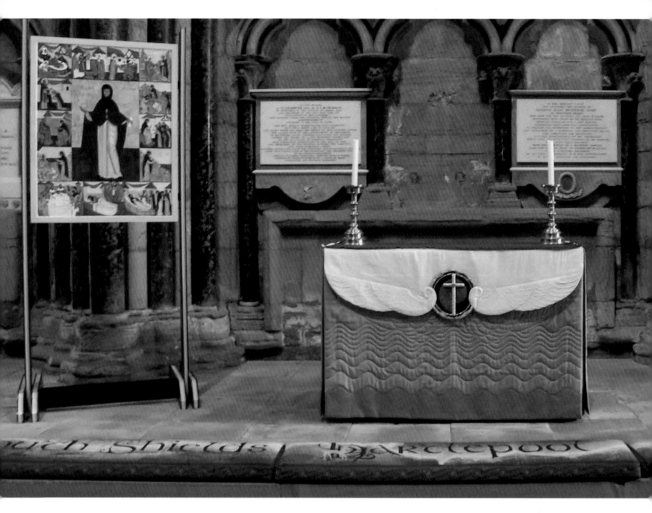

Hild was a seventh century Abbess of Whitby and a contemporary of Aidan and Cuthbert. Born into the royal family, she abandoned the life of the court and entered monastic life. Eventually she was appointed Abbess of Hartlepool by Bishop Aidan. Later she founded the double abbey of monks and nuns at Whitby and was known for her prudence and good sense: kings and other leaders sought her advice. The Synod of Whitby was held at her monastery in 663 when divisive issues between the Celtic and Roman Christian traditions were resolved, most significantly that of the date of Easter which was celebrated at different times in the two traditions. Many of her monks became bishops or scholars of Scripture.

She is also remembered for encouraging a shepherd boy, Caedmon, to become the first English-language poet. Hild, who was universally known as "mother", died in 680 and is remembered as one of the most significant women in the English church, which welcomed the ministry of women.

The altar frontal depicts the sea and seabirds, both regularly associated with St Hild due to her years as abbess at Hartlepool and at Whitby which are sited on promontories overlooking the sea. The cloth represents the sea and is worked in various shot blue silks to suggest the tides and the play of light on the surface of the water.

The technique used is traditional Durham quilting where the linear elements are drawn into running stitch. A natural white cloth over the blue cloth represents the wings of sea birds flying which, tradition tells us, dipped their wings in salute to Hild as they flew over the abbey at Whitby. The wings are symbolic of divine mission and follow the shapes of birds in Celtic art. They may suggest a Goose which has long been associated with providence and vigilance and, in the tradition of the Northern saints, can also represent the Wild Goose, the Holy Spirit.

Others may see in the wings a dove - symbolising purity, peace and the Holy Spirit who descended on Jesus in the form of a dove.

The wings support a silver cross framed by a gold and blue nimbus and implied ammonite, the symbol of St Hild, who is supposed to have transformed snakes into ammonites. The ammonite and wings use bias-cut silk. The silver wing tips and the central silver cross represent a precious metal tested by fire that has become a symbol of purity and chastity, both associated with St Hild. The Psalmist sings, "The promises of the Lord are promises that are pure, silver refined in a furnace on the ground, purified seven times" (Psalm 12:6).

The three kneelers represent the sea and the coastline from South Shields, through Hartlepool, to Whitby. The sea carries the colour from the frontal and the sands have silver wave volutes representing the breakers at the coastline. The names of the three towns associated with St Hild are intended to appear as a vision shining from below to the surface of the water. The canvas stitchery on the land adds a ruggedness to it. Each initial letter contains a symbol associated with St Hild – for example, the hart contemplating the sea and the religious house in Hartlepool to which Hild was appointed by Aidan in 649.

The altar frontal and kneelers were designed by Malcolm Lochhead and worked by the Cathedral Broderers using a variety of techniques. Malcolm Lochhead studied at Glasgow School of Art and is now Millennium Fellow of Design at Glasgow Caledonian University. In addition to his ecclesiastical work, he is involved in community embroidery projects involving large

numbers of people. The Hild Altar was dedicated in November 1999.

The Icon of St Hild is unusual in showing thirteen scenes from the life of a western saint in the art of the eastern church; it is contemporary yet created in the historical tradition of icons. She is shown building the monastery at Whitby; at the Synod held there; offering charity to the poor; encouraging Caedmon; and counselling kings and bishops who sought and heeded her advice.

The icon was written (icons are written, not painted) by Edith Reytiens from Dumfries. She trained with Tom Denny who created the Transfiguration window.

This icon was commissioned by the Community of Women and Men in the Church and the Cathedral Chapter contributed to it. Like the Margaret Altar, the altar dedicated to Hild is part of the Cathedral's intentional expression of the ministry of women.

✠ *We give you thanks, O Lord, for Hild's holiness and leadership which blessed your church in her day. Help us, like her, to yearn for the gospel of Christ and to reconcile those who are divided. This we ask in the name of our Lord Jesus Christ. Amen*

18. The Aidan Altar Frontal

The art in Durham Cathedral illustrates not only biblical stories but also stories of Christians through the ages, including several of the Northern saints who lived in this area in previous centuries.

Aidan was Bishop of Northumbria. He had come to Lindisfarne from Iona at the request of King Oswald of Northumbria and, with his fellow monks, restored Christianity in Northumbria and extended the mission further south. He was known for his generosity to the poor and once gave to a beggar a horse the king had given him, preferring to walk rather than ride through the countryside. It was a vision on the night of Aidan's death in 651 which inspired Cuthbert to enter monastic life.

This altar frontal celebrates the three Northern saints: Aidan, Cuthbert and Bede, by illustrating elements of their lives, and also the bringing of the gospel to Northumbria. It was designed by Leonard Childs, embroidered by the Cathedral Broderers, and dedicated in October 1993, having been given by the Friends of Durham Cathedral.

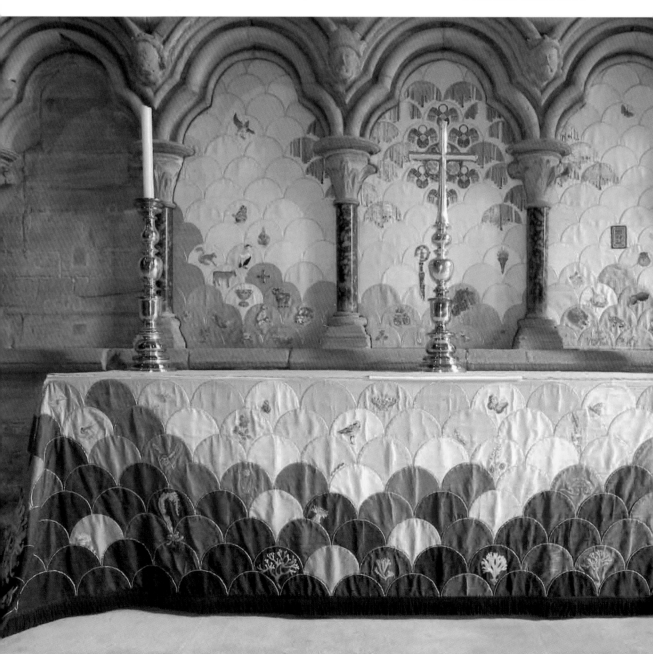

The frontal is said to represent the sea round Lindisfarne, the earth and the sky; some people also say that it also represents humans coming from darkness into light through the resurrection of Christ.

The left panel celebrates St Cuthbert who died in 687. If you look carefully you will see his pectoral

cross, otters – which Bede tells us warmed and dried his feet after he stood in the sea to pray – and eider ducks which were his special friends. The chalice reminds us of his love of the Eucharist. The central panel commemorates Aidan – the ball of fire carries him to paradise, accompanied by angels. The staff represents his calling to be Bishop of the Northumbrians and other details allude to episodes from his life, including the horse he gave away. The right panel celebrates the Venerable Bede who died in 735 and was the greatest scholar of his day. The bottle of ink and the book remind us of his legacy as a biblical scholar, mathematician, historian and biographer of Cuthbert.

Surrounding these symbols of the lives of the three great Northern saints there are birds and flowers of Lindisfarne where Aidan founded a ministry and Cuthbert was later Bishop. You can find a crab, a skylark, a grass snake and seaweed.

There is a cat with a fierce red tongue and a wolf, one of the wild animals Cuthbert would have dealt with when he was a shepherd. There is also a reminder of the sanctuary knocker on the north door.

In an age when we are all too aware of the delicate ecological balance in our world, this altar frontal is both a celebration of the goodness and variety of nature, and a challenge to be good stewards of God's world.

Thank you, O God, for the wonder and variety of your creation and for the skill of scientists in discovering yet more new forms of life in your world. Truly, O Lord, your creation is wonderful. Thank you for the joy of exploring it. Amen.

Malcolm, Margaret and eight of their children appear in the Durham Liber Vitae, the book of donors to the Cathedral.

Malcolm and their oldest son, Edward, were killed in battle at Alnwick fighting King William II of England. Margaret heard the news on 16th November 1093; she died while reciting the communion prayer, supposedly of a broken heart. She was canonised in 1249.

Dame Paula Rego was born in Lisbon in 1935 and has lived in Britain since 1951. This work was commissioned by the Cathedral Chapter and is pastel on paper, mounted on aluminium. St Margaret's left hand points to her most treasured Gospel Book (now in the Bodleian Library). Her right hand rests on the shoulder of her son, David, who is torn between motherly advice and the bravado of the battle-axe and helmet. David later became King and founded many border abbeys. Her ascetic frame and deep penetrating, reflective eyes convey the full force of her personality: this is a woman whose spirituality is wise, tough, discerning and far-sighted. It is not a comfortable image, which portrays the steely, tenacious discipleship that was necessary in those turbulent days. It fits well in a building which stands for a perspective on life lived not simply for the day but in the light of eternity.

The picture in the Chapel of the Nine Altars shows Queen Margaret (c1045-93) with her son who became King David I of Scotland.

Known for her piety, Margaret was born in Hungary, was at the court of Edward the Confessor but in 1068 fled from the Norman court. She was shipwrecked off the Scottish coast, taken in by King Malcolm III and married him, abandoning her intended monastic vocation. She was deeply pious, frequently giving her husband's money to beggars. Eventually she won over her husband, who joined her caring for the poor, sometimes serving nearly 300 needy citizens in their great hall in Dunfermline. Margaret built monasteries and churches, including a new Benedictine abbey at Dunfermline.

Malcolm was present when the foundations of Durham Cathedral were laid in August 1093 and Margaret may have attended the ceremony but her confessor, Prior Turgot of Durham, records that she was so ill that she could scarcely get out of her bed.

The altar frontal, designed by Malcolm Lochhead, draws on a description of the royal couple:

"[King Malcolm] could not bear that even the bindings of her books should be only of rough leather, and when he found a cunning worker in metals, he would have the covers overlaid with gold and precious stones, and with many a round white perk, fit emblem of his Margaret, the Pearl of Queens. It was one of these precious books, a book of the gospels, which Margaret loved above all the rest. Not only was its jewelled cover a token of the King's love, but also the precious words inside were fitly illuminated with golden letters, and there were pictures of the four Evangelists most fair to look upon."

(Amy Steedman in *Our Island Saints*)

The altar frontal suggests a jewelled and gilded book cover, the gold clasp of which is enriched with jewels and opens to reveal a simple black cross with a heart of pearls at the centre. This alludes to Margaret's greatest treasure, a relic of the true Cross, but there is also a double symbolism to this heart – both the love of Malcolm for Margaret and the concept of the heart as the source of understanding, love, courage, devotion and joy; all of which were exemplified in Queen Margaret.

There are echoes of 1 Samuel 16:7, "The Lord said to Samuel, 'Do not look upon his appearance or on the height of his stature … for the Lord does not see as mortals see; they look on the outward appearance, but the Lord looks on the heart.'"

The three kneelers represent rivers that were important in the life and history of St Margaret, and each flows over its name. The Wear refers to Durham, the Danube to Hungary and the Forth to her crossing at Queensferry into Fife and then Dunfermline. The "T" in "Forth" is a cross, thus echoing the frontal and suggesting the Saint traversing the river. The altar frontal and kneelers were made by the Cathedral Broderers.

The location of the Margaret Altar at the east end of the South Quire Aisle was deliberate, picking up on a reference in the Rites of Durham (1593) that "At the east end of the south alley … there was a most fair rood … the black rood of Scotland wrought in silver and having crowns of gold."

The altar was dedicated to St Margaret of Scotland in 2005 as part of a desire to make women more visible in the Cathedral. Margaret challenges us to steely commitment that can endure the hardships of a turbulent life.

20. The Pietà

A Pietà (Latin *pietas*, meaning pity) is a sculpture, painting or drawing of the dead Christ supported by the Virgin Mary. This is not derived from a biblical account, but we are told that Mary was present at the crucifixion and thus watched her son die the slow, cruel death that crucifixion brought about. This pietà expresses Mary's love and sorrow and reminds us of the cost of her "yes" to God all those years earlier and her faithful commitment to God despite the unjusified suffering of her son. This pietà, by Fenwick Lawson, ARCA, who lives close to the Cathedral, is non-traditional in that Jesus lies at Mary's feet rather than being supported by her.

Lawson made this Pietà from beech wood and brass (some of it from his wife's sewing machine) between 1974 and 1981. He aims to embody both death and resurrection. Death is shown through the brutalised crucified body in which the bruised, bent knees and the dismembered, unformed arm show the history of events. Resurrection and life are expressed through the lifting arm and the dynamic of the hand, stretched out to the mother, recalling Jesus' words from the cross, entrusting his mother to the care of his disciple, "Woman, behold your son", and, "Behold your mother"(John 19:26).

The unpolished brass, which is a vehicle for light and a metaphor for life, is meant to reinforce this and signifies the transfiguration of Christ earlier in his life – even in death, God's light is not extinguished.

The splitting of the wood in the mother's face expresses the trauma of bereavement. She is both Mary, the mother of Jesus, and the universal mother who has contained and given life, now expressing understanding and compassion at the death of her child. She represents all people who have stayed alongside others in their suffering. The outward gesture of her hand offers life, through sacrificial death. This is not the beautiful young Mary of the annunciation, but Mary harrowed by suffering who, nevertheless, sees the horror through to its end, not abandoning her son in his hour of need. Her presence at the cross is an example of discipleship and love that does not count the cost but is shaped by love for others. Mary knows that the only response to crucifixion is faithful lament and the ministry of presence which comforts her son and is a protest against the horror and injustice of the crucifixion.

The Pietà was displayed in this Cathedral in 1984 and was then placed in York Minster where it survived the fire in 1984.

The Christ figure was under burning timber but the mother was saved by a wrought iron screen. They were both splattered with molten lead falling from the roof, which the sculptor sees as enhancing the meaning of this sculpture in a way that he could not have done himself.

The sarcophagus, next to the pietà, is missed by many people. It represents the fourteenth station of the cross in traditional devotion, and was carved from oak and bronze in 1985. Like the pieta, it offers a duality of meaning with the wood of the felled tree displaying the image of death, accentuated by the cut of the chainsaw, while the bronze elements on the head and hands are a vehicle for light, a metaphor for life, thus signifying the resurrection.

Fenwick Lawson was born in 1932 in South Moor, Co. Durham and grew up in Craghead. While studying at Sunderland College of Art and The Royal College of Art he was influenced by Jacob Epstein. A scholarship allowed him to travel in Europe experiencing the work of the masters, including Michelangelo and Donatello, and Cycladic art which led to his interest in its simplicity of form. He was Head of the Sculpture department at Newcastle Polytechnic until he retired from teaching in 1984. He continues to create works of art which reflect the area's spiritual life and history, including *The Journey*, now on Holy Island, which was cast in bronze and placed in Durham's Millennium Place in 2008 and shows six monks carrying Cuthbert's coffin towards its final resting place in Durham Cathedral.

Be present, Lord Jesus, with people who weep in their sorrow.
Strengthen those who sit beside people as they suffer, and bring
them the comfort and strength of your presence with them.
We ask this in your name, our saviour and our friend. Amen.

The transfiguration of Christ is recorded in the first three gospels, and is alluded to in one of the epistles. Jesus took three friends up a mountain where he was transfigured and his clothes becoming dazzling white. Elijah and Moses, from the Old Testament, appeared and spoke to him about his coming death. The disciples were terrified. Then a cloud overshadowed them and they heard a voice saying, "This is my Son, the Beloved; listen to him!" Then the vision ended.

The Transfiguration window was given by the Friends of Durham Cathedral in honour of Michael Ramsey, Canon Professor at Durham Cathedral in the 1940s, later Bishop of Durham, Archbishop of York and then Archbishop of Canterbury. It reflects Ramsey's strong theological interest in the theme of "glory". The tapering shaft of white and gold which descends through the window holds the narrative figures of the transfiguration of Christ, echoing Ramsey's own awareness that the Christian always lives in the tension between history and eternity.

The window is full of possible meanings; there is a first impression of light, but look carefully and you will see detailed figures from stories from the Bible and Durham's history.

The six figures at the transfiguration can be seen – Christ, Moses and Elijah and the three watching disciples. Christ's forthcoming crucifixion is suggested in the quatrefoil at the top of the window.

Look more carefully and you will find, at the bottom, the healing of the epileptic boy which immediately followed the transfiguration, while another scene of human suffering speaks of the power of darkness into which Christ's glory shines. There are also scenes of new life – two figures run, accompanied by an eagle, echoing the words, "Bless the Lord … who crowns you with steadfast love and mercy, who satisfies you with good as long as you live, so that your youth is renewed like the eagle's."(Psalm 103:1,4,5)

The eagle is also associated with St Cuthbert who appears above it, keeping prayerful night watch accompanied by the splash of waves.

The Cathedral can be seen above a wooded valley with figures walking to it on pilgrimage, echoing the encounter on the road to Emmaus. The artist has made one of these pilgrims look like Ramsey.

The window was designed and made by Tom Denny, a stained glass artist from Dorset who has created windows for several churches, including Sunderland Minster. He has worked with layers of flashed glass, acid etched to make tonal modulations and create new colours, some of which are silver stained and some painted. The window was dedicated on 25th September 2010.

Lord Jesus Christ, shine your light on our hearts and in our world today, especially in the needy places where there is suffering. We pray this in your name. Amen.

22. The Millennium Window

The Millennium window brings the history of the modern world into dialogue with the history of this region, especially St Cuthbert on whom the top half of the window focuses. There are scenes from Holy Island where he lived - the coffin of the saint being taken from there when the threat of invasion by the Danes in 875 forced the remaining monks to flee, and of Chester-le-Street, where his body rested for 107 years before being brought to Durham.

The lower half of the window illustrates contemporary life in the region, including glass-blowing, ship-building, chemicals, car manufacture and coal-mining: all linked to shipping, shown by the Tyne Bridge, and railways, shown by Stephenson's 1825 Locomotion engine which reminds us that railways are a gift of County Durham to the world, beginning just a few miles south of here.

The mining industry is now no longer active in Durham although the legacy lives on in the villages across the County and is expressed annually in the Miners' Gala. The church's engagement with society is illustrated by the two pictures showing Bishop Westcott - the Bishop of Durham at the end of the nineteenth century who is remembered as the "Miners' Bishop" and helped to bring resolution to the 1892 miners' strike - reaching out to shake the hand of a miner. Durham University, founded in 1832 by Bishop van Mildert and the Dean and Chapter of Durham, is represented by a 1990s computer printing out the account of the removal of St Cuthbert's relics from Chester-le-Street to Durham, as recorded by the 12th century monk, Simeon. The rural nature of much of the County and its farming heritage is portrayed in the pastoral scene.

Joseph Nuttgens has designed and made stained glass since near High Wycombe since 1982. This Millennium window in the South Quire Aisle was dedicated on 22nd March 1997 to celebrate the millennium anniversary, in 1993, of the arrival of the shrine of St Cuthbert at Durham and the foundation of the Diocese. The glass comes from the Sunderland firm of Hartley Wood and the glazier is Bernard Seaton. It is largely transparent and on sunny days the colours play on the stonework of the South Quire Aisle. The window was commissioned in memory of Robert Tobias Binks (d 1959) and his wife Jane Watson (d1934) who lived in Thornley, Co. Durham. The brief specified a representational window showing life in County Durham.

Thank you, O God, for the places where we live and for the variety of our heritage in the region. We offer you our own daily life and work, and pray for those who are unemployed or in demeaning work. Help us to use our skills and creativity for the good of all people. We ask this in the name of Jesus Christ, who once worked at a carpenter's bench. Amen.

This Cathedral is dedicated to St Cuthbert – the dedication, having been removed by Henry VIII at the Reformation, was restored in 2005. Cuthbert, who died in 687, is closely connected with St Oswald who died in 642 since they not only share the same burial place – Oswald's head was placed in Cuthbert's tomb in 875 – but were connected in life through St Aidan whom Oswald, King of Northumbria, brought from Iona and whose death led Cuthbert to become a missionary.

The Cuthbert and Oswald batik banners in the Feretory are by Thetis Blacker who used wax from candle stubs at the votive candle stands in the Cathedral – they are literally an offering of prayer. Oswald, who was converted while in exile on Iona, defeated a pagan army at the battle of Heavenfield, but died in another battle in 642. The ambiguities of Christian history and war are shown as Oswald advances towards us with raised sword, inscribed *Pro Pace* ("for peace"), with the cross of Heavenfield in the background.

The Flanders poppies show war's tragic cost. The raven and dove, with their faces turned towards St Cuthbert's tomb, are messengers between heaven and earth. The raven, which is repeated in the two beaten metal finials on the top of the banner (made by Peter Sales), can be associated with war but is counterbalanced by the dove of peace; the ambivalence of the two is a reminder to hold before God all who, like Oswald, strive through arms to bring about a greater peace.

The silver platter with twelve loaves on it illustrates Oswald's generosity to the poor and it is fragmented by cracks because he broke it and gave the fragments to the poor. The well (with a dove of peace representing the Holy Spirit) alludes to the healing power Oswald exercised on a poor woman and a sick horse, among others. Together the bread and the well water point us to the Christian symbols of the healing water of baptism and the life-giving bread of the Eucharist.

Cuthbert is shown as a bishop, serving the people entrusted to him. He wears a mitre, carries a bishop's staff and raises his hand in blessing. He is being fed a salmon by an eagle, recalling the stories of his trusting relationship with wild animals and also the early Christian use of the symbolism of a fish to signify Christ: the letters of the Greek word for fish (*ichthus*) abbreviate "Jesus Christ, Son of God and Saviour": Christ gave his life for us and we share his body and blood in the Eucharist.

The artist painted the eye of the Fish crimson - as are the garnets of St Cuthbert's Cross - the colour of blood, of wine, of sacrifice. The eagle points to the promise that those who trust in the Lord will "mount up with wings like eagles" (Isaiah 40:31).

Blacker painted St Cuthbert's vestments according to a description of how they would have been in the seventh century. The green of his chasuble would have been a bluey-green; his mitre would not have

been pointed, as in later depictions, but high and rounded. His crozier would have been curved over and pointed outwards and his hair would have been tonsured under his mitre; his face ascetic and clean-shaven. His eyes radiate light and compassion, reflecting the ocean and the sky.

Blacker painted a sea otter and a seal emerging from the waters unafraid before the saint. On the right, the great eagle has caught the salmon offered to St Cuthbert.

Blacker wrote that the whole picture is covered with spots and sparkles of light and water, while Cuthbert's halo radiates outwards, unbounded and his pectoral cross also radiates light. She also said that she tried to show in St Oswald that sacrifice and suffering of war lead to eventual reconciliation, peace and healing, and in St Cuthbert that wholeness comes through faith, sacrifice, strength, and reverence for all living things.

These banners were donated by Henry Dyson and Alan Richards, Fellows of Grey College in Durham, and dedicated at Pentecost 2001.

Loving Father, whom the whole company of the saints adore: we rejoice with all our hearts in Cuthbert, glory of our sanctuary and ever-living symbol of our apostleship. Help us to follow his example by the simplicity of our lives and by the power of our witness, through Jesus Christ our Lord. Amen

*With the Holy Spirit,
In the glory of God
the Father. Amen.*

Sir Ninian Comper (1864-1960), the creator of the canopy, was born in Aberdeen and trained as an architect. His hallmark is the use of vibrant colour which can be seen in this canopy with its strong clear blocks of blue, rose and gold dominating the ceiling for anyone who looks up from Cuthbert's simple shrine.

Comper believed that churches should be not only functional but also beautiful and that architecture should embody and aid liturgical worship: his art was never made for its own sake. When designing a church, which he believed was "a roof over an altar", he designed and built from the altar outwards. Sir John Betjeman once said of him, "His ecclesiastical tastes are rococo... He is perfectly satisfied so long as gold leaf is heaped on everywhere." It is used to great effect in this location, shimmering with heaven's glory over the tomb of one of earth's saints.

After Jesus Christ was raised from the dead, he appeared to his disciples for forty days and then returned to heaven, where Christians believe he is seated at God's right hand. The canopy, or tester, over the shrine of St Cuthbert depicts Christ in glory, reigning over the world. At the four corners, the four Gospel writers with their symbols point to their texts which tell us the story of Christ's life, death and resurrection.

The juxtaposition of the monochrome simplicity of Cuthbert's memorial comprising a stone slab with only his name carved on it, with the colourful and intricate portrayal of Christ seated on a hidden throne, surrounded by angels and shafts of golden glory radiating outwards to the four evangelists, is a brilliant artistic interpretation of theological truth: Cuthbert, the North-East's beloved saint, is overshadowed by the glory of Jesus Christ, whom he served so lovingly.

This artistic representation shows Christ beardless, as in the tradition of some early Hellenistic Christian depictions of him as the eternal youth, now enthroned in glory. It conveys in art the theme of one of the earliest Christian hymns still sung today, the Gloria:

*Lord Jesus Christ,
only Son of the Father,
Lord God, Lamb of God,
You take away the sin
of the world:
Have mercy on us;
You are seated at the
right hand of the Father:
Receive our prayer.
For you alone are the Holy
One,
You are alone are the Lord,
You alone are the Most
High, Jesus Christ,*

The wires which hold up this painting go through the same holes in the vault through which the ropes which held the medieval shrine cover passed, and the painting can be raised and lowered as the original shrine cover was, although this rarely happens.

Pray the words of the Gloria, thus joining in one of the earliest Christian hymns.